T0196413

MOVING OUT FROM THE PEW: EQUIPPING THE SAINTS FOR THE WORK OF MINISTRY

A Training Manual For Lay Leaders

REV. DR. CONNIE WELCH

WESTBOW
P R E S S®
A DIVISION OF THOMAS NELSON
& ZONDERVAN

WestBow Press books may be ordered through booksellers or by contacting:

WestBow Press
A Division of Thomas Nelson & Zondervan
1663 Liberty Drive
Bloomington, IN 47403
www.westbowpress.com
1 (866) 928-1240

Because of the dynamic nature of the Internet, any web addresses or links contained in this book may have changed since publication and may no longer be valid. The views expressed in this work are solely those of the author and do not necessarily reflect the views of the publisher, and the publisher hereby disclaims any responsibility for them.

Any people depicted in stock imagery provided by Thinkstock are models, and such images are being used for illustrative purposes only.
Certain stock imagery © Thinkstock.

ISBN: 978-1-5127-6703-2 (sc)
ISBN: 978-1-5127-6702-5 (e)

Library of Congress Control Number: 2016919931

Print information available on the last page.

WestBow Press rev. date: 1/3/2017

TABLE OF CONTENTS

ACKNOWLEDGMENTS

First, I must thank my God for giving me the grace to complete this book. To Dr. Quentin Newhouse Jr., you are truly a godsend! Words cannot express how grateful I am for your support, Godly counsel, friendship, and spiritual discernment. I wish you only the very best in life! To Dr. Mary Young, thank you so much for your esteemed guidance, your continued support, your time, and your friendship! You are the best! To Bishop Vince McLaughlin, I will always be eternally grateful to you for affording me my first position as a college professor. Without the three of you, this book would not have been possible. To my father, Rev. Leon W. Baylor, and my mother, the late Elsie K. Baylor, I can't thank you enough. You both planted the seed, and you watered it! There are no words to express my gratitude to my sons, Justin and Jason, and my daughter-in-law, Ariel. As my dad would say to me, "You make life worth living!" You're my best friends and my biggest supporters! You have taught me more than you could ever imagine! To the Connie Welch Ministries and Emmanuel Christian Institute families, thank you both for your undying support and faithfulness. The best is yet to come! And thank you to my beloved, compassionate pit bull, Gracie. You continue to remain at my side all night and during the early morning hours. Both you and I defy all stereotypes and labels man has tried to place on us! You have been faithful to the end.

Lastly, but most importantly, a special note of thanks to my readers! This training manual is designed to preach and teach to the whole house! I pray that all of you will be able to take something from this training, and use it greatly as you continue on your Christian journey.

To God be the glory for what He has done!

INTRODUCTION

This is a transformational training course designed for church leaders of various educational backgrounds. It is an intense training program that teaches the basic interpretive, homiletic, and public speaking skills necessary to prepare lay leaders and to move them forward in the work of the ministry. The course is divided into thirty-three sessions, with the length of each session to be determined by the instructor.

The course contains four major components or modules: (1) biblical interpretation methodology and skills, (2) homiletical skills in drafting and delivering a sermon and/or a Bible study/Sunday school lesson, (3) public speaking skills, and (4) leadership skills. It is recommended that the students also keep a journal throughout the entire course to record their thoughts and revelations as they spend time meditating in the Word and in God's presence.

It is the overarching goal that at the end of this course, the students will have learned the fundamental biblical interpretation skills necessary to "rightly explain the word of truth,"[1] and the homiletical skills necessary to be able to articulate the truth in such a way that their preaching and teaching will have a much more profound impact on those listening to the sound of their voices.

---

[1] 2 Timothy 2:15 (NRSV).

MODULAR OVERVIEW

Module 1: Biblical Interpretation

The biblical interpretation module is designed to teach the students exegetical skills in interpreting a biblical text. Students are taught to examine the historical, literary, and cultural aspects of the text. They are taught to critically examine the text and to be suspicious of the text. At the end of this module, the students will have acquired the necessary fundamental tools to conduct a thorough exegesis. The main objective for this module is for the students to have a deeper and more thorough understanding of the meaning of a text by having the skills necessary to interpret it. At the end of this module, the students will be evaluated by two methods: (1) by taking a test designed to assess their understanding of biblical interpretation terminology and, (2) by performing an exegesis of a particular scripture using the skill set that they learned from this course.

Teacher/Student Objectives

The teacher objectives of this module are:

- to illustrate fundamental biblical interpretation skills to be used when interpreting scripture;
- to instruct the students on how to conduct an exegesis of a biblical text by examining the historical, literary, and cultural contexts; and
- to demonstrate how to integrate principles of biblical interpretation when conducting an exegesis from scriptures of various translations of the Bible.

The student objectives of this module are:

- to obtain a deeper understanding of the Word of God through the use of basic biblical interpretation skills;
- to become familiar with biblical interpretation terminology and methodology; and
- to be able to examine the historical, literary, and cultural contexts of scriptures from various translations of the Bible.

Textbooks/Other Resources

In this module, the main texts used are *How to Read the Bible for all Its Worth*, by Gordon Fee and Douglas Stuart; and *Living by the Book*, by Howard G. Hendricks and William D. Hendricks. In *How to Read the Bible for all Its Worth*, the authors write:

> Because the Bible is *God's Word*, it has *eternal relevance;* it speaks to all humankind, in every age and in every culture. But because God chose to speak his Word through human words in history, every book in the Bible also has historical particularity; each document is conditioned by the language, time, and culture in which it was originally written (and in some cases also by the oral history it had before it was written down). Interpretation of the Bible is demanded by the "tension" that exists between its *eternal relevance* and its *historical particularity.*[2]

Students should be instructed to look at the text contextually by examining its historical, cultural, and literary contexts. They should also be instructed to use the following resources when performing an exegesis of a text:

> *New Interpreter's Bible and Commentary* (twelve-volume set, 2003)
> Logos Bible Software
> *New Oxford Annotated Bible, w/Apocrypha,* new revised version (4th ed., 2010)

This is a hands-on course. PowerPoint presentations and handouts are provided as references and to facilitate classroom discussions. In addition, it is recommended that a blackboard or smart board be used during class instruction for illustrations. Class time should consist of all these methods, along with discussions among the students and the instructor. Presentation materials are to be given through lectures outlining the principles of biblical interpretation, utilizing an inductive methodical approach to studying the scriptures. Previous student exegetical work conducted by this author while attending seminary is also provided as examples to follow when conducting an exegesis of a text.

Classroom Instruction/Lesson Plan

As a class, begin with an exegetical eye studying the book of Mark, because it is the shortest of the Gospels and the first one written. As a first step in the exegetical process, the students should be taught to look at the text in its historical context. This also takes into account the autobiographical and cultural aspects of the author and the audience, as well as the relevant geographical, topographical, and political factors of that time.

Begin with the prophetic conversation between God and Jesus in the first few verses of

---

[2] Gordon Fee and Douglas Stuart, *How to Read the Bible for all Its Worth* (Grand Rapids, MI: Zondervan, 2003), 21. Used by permission of Zondervan.

Mark chapter 1. Discuss the importance of knowing who is speaking and who is being spoken to. Discuss the importance of the connector words "and so" in verse 4 of Mark chapter 1. In this same vein, continue to look at select scriptures within the book of Mark, establishing if there are any constant themes throughout a particular chapter (i.e., the teachings of Jesus) and identifying key people, places, and words (i.e., "Son of Man,"[3] "Kingdom of God").[4]

Begin to study the other parts of the Bible by studying Old Testament narratives, Psalms, the prophetic books, and the Epistles. After conducting several exegetical exercises as a class, the students should be divided into groups. Give each group a different scripture from one of the translations to conduct an exegesis of that particular text.

With regard to studying the literary context of a particular text, guidance is given by Hendricks and Hendricks concerning the fourteen genres of the Bible: apocalyptic, biography, encomium, exposition, narrative, oratory, parable, pastoral, poetry, prophecy, proverb, satire, tragedy, and wisdom literature.[5] The class should discuss the five keys to interpretation: content, context, comparison, culture, and consultation.[6] In addition, students should apply the interrogative questions to each text: who wrote it, when was it written, where did it occur, what was happening at the time to inspire the text to be written, and why was it written? And finally, with the interrogatives, they should also ask the nine questions Hendricks proposes we ask ourselves when studying scripture:[7]

- Is there an example for me to follow?
- Is there a sin to avoid?
- Is there a promise to claim?
- Is there a prayer to repeat?
- Is there a command to obey?
- Is there a condition to meet?
- Is there a verse to memorize?
- Is there an error to mark?
- Is there a challenge to face?

Student Evaluation/Assessment

At the end of this module, the students should be given an exam (an example is provided), and time should be allotted for them to conduct a short exegetical exercise, demonstrating what they learned.

---

[3] Mark 2:10 (NIV).

[4] Mark 1:15 (NIV).

[5] Howard G. Hendricks and William D. Hendricks, *Living by the Book, the Art and Science of Reading the Bible* (Chicago: Moody Publishers, 2007), 224–26. Used by permission of Moody Publishers.

[6] Ibid., 227.

[7] Ibid., 342.

Module 2: Homiletics

Now that the students have been introduced to fundamental biblical interpretation skills, the next goal is to be able to take what they have learned and present it in such a way that it speaks to the hearts and souls of their audiences. Emphasis is placed on relating what they have learned about the text to today's audience, so those who are listening can hear what God is saying to them through the voice of the preacher/teacher. This is done by (1) taking the biblical knowledge they have acquired through conducting a careful exegesis of the text, (2) presenting it in the main body by using a limited number of main points, and (3) taking those main points and through life examples, apply them to the lives of the believers.

Teacher/Student Objectives

The teacher objectives are:

- to demonstrate the developmental stages in preaching and teaching preparation,
- to illustrate how to apply information obtained through the exegetical process to today's listeners, and
- to illustrate the parts of a sermon.

The student objectives are:

- to learn how to put together an effective sermon,
- to learn how to take information obtained from conducting an exegesis and transform it into a sermon or biblical teaching, and
- to learn how to apply the information obtained through the exegesis of a text and make it applicable to today's listeners.

Textbooks/Other Resources

The suggested texts for this module are *The Art of Preaching Old Testament Narrative* (Mathewson, 2002) and *Christ-Centered Preaching, Redeeming the Expository Sermon* (Chapell, 2005). These texts give excellent instruction regarding biblical preaching and application. In *The Art of Preaching Old Testament Narrative*, students learn the art of storytelling and how it can have a major impact on relating the sermon to the audience. Mathewson also instructs the reader to look for the protagonist, antagonist, and the foil when studying and preaching from an Old Testament story, and to relate the actions and personalities of each one to the purpose of the story.[8]

---

[8] Steven D. Mathewson, *The Art of Preaching Old Testament Narrative* (Grand Rapids, MI: Baker Academic, 2002), 58.

Classroom Instruction/Lesson Plan

Students are given the definition of a sermon: "a sermon, then, must be a statement of faith, drawn from the context of the tradition and projecting the authentic being of the preacher."[9] Chapell defines the expository sermon as "a message whose structure and thought are derived from a biblical text, that covers the scope of the text, and that explains the features and context of the text in order to disciple the enduring principles for faithful thinking, living, and worship intended by the Holy Spirit, who inspired the text."[10]

According to Chapell, in preparing a sermon, the preacher must ask six critical questions:[11]

- What does the text mean?
- How do I know what the text means?
- What concerns caused the text to be written?
- What do we share in common with those to (or about) whom the text was written and/ or the one by whom the text was written?
- How should people now respond to the truths of the text?
- What is the most effective way I can communicate the meaning of the text?

Chapell states, "prior to answering these questions, a preacher has information only about a text, not a sermon."[12] During this preparation, attention is given to the principle of the fallen condition focus (FCF). According to Chapell, the purpose of the text, as well as the purpose of the sermon, is revealed by the FCF. He defines the FCF as the "mutual human condition that contemporary believers share with those to or about whom the text was written that requires the grace of the passage for God's people to glorify and enjoy him."[13] Therefore, specific aspects of a text address a human problem or burden.

Together, as a class, discuss certain texts and apply the six critical questions that Chapell directs us to ask. The texts can be chosen from any genre of the Bible. In addition to applying the six critical questions, also determine the fallen condition focus (FCF) as it relates to the text. The FCF does not always have to be a specific sin (i.e., greed, lust, rebellion, etc.). It can be grief, illness, parental guidance, determining God's will, etc. Using Mathewson's *The Art of Preaching Old Testament Narrative*, discuss sermon preparation using an Old Testament narrative text. Identify the protagonist, the antagonist, and the foil. In identifying the purpose of the sermon and the text, ask the following questions proposed by Chapell:[14]

---

[9] James M. Wall, "The Sermon: A Work of Art," *The Christian Ministry* 7/6 (November 1976): 28.

[10] Bryan Chapell, *Christ-Centered Preaching, Redeeming the Expository Sermon* (Grand Rapids, MI: Baker Academic, 2005), 31. Used by permission of Baker Academic.

[11] Ibid., 104–5.

[12] Ibid., 105.

[13] Chapell, 50. Used by permission of Baker Academic.

[14] Ibid., 52.

- What does the text say?
- What spiritual concerns did the text address?
- What spiritual concerns do listeners share in common with those to (or about) whom the text is written?

The students should be taught the basic parts of a sermon—the introduction, the main body, and the conclusion. Sermon application should be emphasized heavily in this module. Without application, the audience is left with knowledge of what was going on at that time, but with no instruction as to how to apply it to their own lives.

As a class, look at several scriptures together; conduct an exegesis of the text, and then relate the text to today's audience. This is done several times together as a class, after which the class should be divided into smaller groups, and the exercise should be repeated. Regarding each scripture, the students must answer the six critical questions posed by Chapell. The students should also draft an introduction and a closing for each text studied in the class or within their smaller group.

Student Evaluation/Assessment

Students are evaluated on what they have learned in this module by preaching a sermon or teaching a Bible study lesson. Students should choose a scripture with wisdom, taking into consideration the allotted time (ten to fifteen minutes) and complexity of the text. Using various biblical study tools, the students should be reminded to look at the historical, cultural, and literary context of the scripture. After careful exegesis, the students should be encouraged to construct an outline of the sermon, consisting of the introduction, background, main points and subpoints, application, and conclusion.

After the sermons/lessons are given, the class as a whole gives constructive written and oral feedback by affirming what the student did well and suggesting areas of improvement. The written feedback is done using the Speech Evaluation Form[15] (appendix E). The sermons should be conducted after the leadership module, and they should be videotaped. Each student should be allotted ten to fifteen minutes to speak. This practice not only forces the student to be organized in his or her sermon, but it also reinforces the fact that the length of a sermon does not determine its effectiveness. Sermon outlines are to be turned in to the instructor before preaching. Students may discuss their scripture and exegetical work with the instructor prior to speaking if they have questions or need further guidance. At the end of the class, each student is shown his or her videoed sermon to evaluate his or her own personal growth and to determine areas of improvement regarding his or her public speaking skills.

---

[15] Stephen E. Lucas, *The Art of Public Speaking, Instructor's Manual* (New York: McGraw Hill, 2009) 50. Used by permission of Stephen E. Lucas.

Module 3: Public Speaking Skills

Public speaking skills are taught during the third module. Now that the students are armed with biblical interpretation skills, and now that they have a feel for how to put a sermon or lesson together, they will be instructed on how to deliver the sermon/lesson. In this module, the methods of persuasion, as well as delivery techniques, are taught. Also during this module, a general debate is held that will allow the students to cultivate their persuasion skills. Students should be taught the methods of persuasion (i.e., the Monroe sequence), and then given an opportunity to demonstrate what they have learned by debating for or against controversial topics and/or current events: for example, pro-choice, and gay/lesbian pastors and church leaders. The instructor and/or an outside judge determines the winners of the debate. The debates should be videotaped.

Teacher/Student Objectives

The teacher objectives are:

- to demonstrate how to organize, write, and deliver various types of speeches;
- to demonstrate how to apply communication theories when speaking before an audience; and
- to demonstrate basic speech delivery skills.

The student objectives are:

- to learn how to organize and transform thoughts and ideas into an effective speech and/or sermon, and
- to learn presentation and communication skills that can be used to give a speech or a sermon.

Textbook/Other Resources

The textbook for this module is entitled *The Art of Public Speaking* (Lucas, 10th ed., 2009).

Classroom Instruction/Lesson Plan

In this module, we focus on the method of persuasion as a form of public speaking. As preachers and teachers of the Gospel, our role is to persuade (not manipulate) our audience to accept Jesus, to desire a closer walk with Him, and to repent of their sins. Lucas states that "persuasion is the process of creating, reinforcing, or changing people's beliefs or actions."[16]

---

[16] Ibid., 324–25.

We are advocates for Jesus Christ. As advocates, we try to persuade our listeners through sound doctrine by using methods of persuasion. In this module, students study the four patterns of organization used in persuasive speeches: (1) the problem-solution order, (2) the problem-cause-solution order, (3) the comparative advantages order, and (4) the Monroe's motivated sequence order.

During this module, the students view the movie *The Great Debaters*. It is based on a true story, and is centered on the debate team at Wiley College, a historical black college located in the South. The debate coach pushes to get his team recognized by predominantly white schools, and eventually the team has a chance to debate against Harvard University (in the true story it was actually the University of Southern California). The movie not only depicts the hard work of the members of the debate team, but the story lines also show life in the rural South during the Jim Crow era. This movie was chosen to illustrate to the students how a team debate is conducted and the power of persuasive speaking. It also demonstrates that, in addition to conducting research on a particular topic, life experiences are also key, and can have a major impact when trying to relate to the audience and in emphasizing a particular point.

Debate topics should be chosen by the instructor and should be controversial in nature (i.e., homosexuality in the church, abortion, etc.) and/or related to real time world events. The students will have to conduct research on their particular topic to be able to argue their position for or against it. Students should be encouraged to use statistics, news articles, and other information from reliable sources to support their positions. The students are allowed to use scriptures but should be directed to not rely solely on them. The intent is for the students to gain experience in researching information from various sources. Two teams should be set up, with one team arguing in support of a particular topic and the other team arguing against it. The number of teams and topics to be debated is dependent upon the size of the class. Team members will be given a certain amount of time to present their arguments regarding their team's topic and to counterargue with their opponent. As illustrated in the movie, each team chooses a captain. The instructor chooses which team will debate first, after which the team chooses what team member will go first to give the opening remarks. At the end of the debate, each team presents closing arguments. Winners should be chosen based on their use of the persuasion techniques discussed in class.

Also discussed in this module are delivery and presentation skills. Students learn the parts of a speech: (1) the introduction, (2) main points, and (3) the conclusion. The students also learn the relevance of each part and how to capitalize on each part of the speech in order to be effective. Regarding delivery of the speech, students learn basic delivery skills such as: (1) maintaining eye contact with the audience, (2) refraining from vocalized pauses (i.e., umm, uh), (3) using vocal variety, and (4) communicating enthusiasm.

Student Evaluation/Assessment

The debates should be videotaped, and should be shown to the students at the end of the class. The debates are conducted before the students preach in order to give all of the students some prior public speaking experience. In addition to hearing the instructor's and/or judge's comments, the students are allowed to critique each other on their performances, use of their persuasion skills and techniques, and their delivery skills. This strategy prepares them for preaching at the end of the class. Some students will have had previous public speaking experience outside of the church, and some will not. Also at the end of the course, students should view the videos of both their debate presentations and their sermons. Each student is shown his or her own videotaped presentation and sermonic message so that they can see for themselves how much they have grown from the beginning of the class in their public speaking capabilities, their spiritual development, and their biblical knowledge and interpretive skills.

Module 4: Leadership

During the last module, leadership skills are taught. Various leadership styles are discussed. The students should be asked if they can identify their own current leadership style, and the leadership style they aspire to have. In this module, the students also study how various leaders in the Bible responded to their own leadership calls.

Teacher/Student Objectives

The teacher objectives are:

- to instruct the students concerning the characteristics of an effective leader;
- to instruct the students concerning the various leadership styles, the pros and cons of each one; and
- to assist them in identifying their own personal leadership styles.

The student objectives are:

- to learn the characteristics of an effective leader,
- to be able to identify individual leadership styles, and
- to understand the pros and cons of various leadership styles.

Textbook/Other Resources

The textbook used for this module is entitled *The 21 Indispensible Qualities of a Leader*, by John C. Maxwell. Other resources used to facilitate the discussions on leadership include a discussion on the various leadership styles as defined by MindTools (www.mindtools.com) and by a PowerPoint presentation entitled "The Makings of An Effective Leader."

Classroom Instruction/Lesson Plan

During this module, John Maxwell's *21 Indispensable Qualities of a Leader* are discussed. Each quality should be discussed as it relates to the students' current leadership positions in the church, as well as in their homes and in their workplaces. Also for discussion are the various types of leadership styles as defined by MindTools,[17] an organization dedicated to management and leadership training. The various leadership styles discussed are:

- Transactional leadership
- Autocratic leadership
- Bureaucratic leadership
- Charismatic leadership
- Democratic/participative leadership
- Laissez-faire leadership
- Task-oriented leadership
- People-oriented leadership
- Servant leadership
- Transformational leadership

The pros and cons of each leadership style, as well as specific situations where each style would be applicable should be discussed and vetted among the students.

The class discusses the differences between a manager and a leader, and the leadership call in general as it relates to being a leader in the church. Time should also be allotted to discuss various leaders in the Bible (i.e., the self-appointed leader and the God-appointed leader), their leadership style, and how they responded to the leadership call on their life (Moses, Jeremiah, and Gideon are discussed in the class handouts). The students should try to identify where they are on their own leadership journey with regard to their preparation phase, not just formal classroom training but in other areas of their lives.

Journal Writing/Transformational Time

Throughout this course, the students are required to keep a journal. The requirement for keeping a journal will increase the writing skills for those students where English is their second language. More importantly, it is a time for the student to spend quality time with God. Each student is expected to select a scripture, meditate and pray, and hear what the Holy Spirit is speaking to him or her regarding that particular scripture. If so desired, the student may

---

[17] MindTools.com, "Leadership styles" [online], available from: http://www.mindtools.com/pages/article/newLDR_84.htm (accessed June 5, 2016). Used by permission of Mindtools.

share his or her thoughts with the class. The journals should be handed in to the instructor on a regular basis to keep track of journal entries and to observe their basic knowledge of the English language. Time will be allotted to discuss with the students their current writing capabilities and offer suggestions for improvement if needed.

Teacher/Student Objectives

The teacher objectives for this exercise are:

- to emphasize to the students the importance of spending quality time with God and quality time meditating on His Word,
- to emphasize the importance of journal writing as a means of communication with God, and
- to engage the student in practicing his or her writing skills.

The student objectives are:

- to spend quality time with God,
- to develop a disciplined life of meditating on the Word of God, and
- to establish a habit of recording thoughts, ideas, and revelations.

The purpose of this exercise is to get the students in the habit of spending alone time with God. Busyness in church can hinder prayer and study time in the Word. This exercise also enables them to grow spiritually by increasing their faith and trust in God. The student is strengthened and encouraged by developing a prayer/meditation life. Though this course emphasizes sermon preparation, by spending time with God, the student is not caught off guard if or when the Holy Spirit directs him or her on a different path, or when called upon to speak at the last minute. They are still equipped to handle the task at hand because they have established a walk with God and have spent quality time in His word, meditating and seeking His will.

Students should be required to record in their journals at least twice a week. They should be directed to meditate on a specific verse of their own choosing, or on a particular issue God has laid on their hearts. They should record any revelations as they meditate and ask the Holy Spirit to speak to them regarding a specific verse or scripture. Students should share their thoughts with the class.

DETAILED LESSON PLANS PER SESSION

The following lesson plans should be used in facilitating the classroom discussions for each session. The length of each session is determined by the instructor, and may consist of one or more scheduled class times. There are a total of thirty-three sessions. These include those sessions strictly devoted to student preaching, the class debates, and planned exit interviews.

Module 1: Biblical Interpretation

Biblical Interpretation (Session 1)

Begin this module by going over the presentation entitled "Principles of Biblical Interpretation" (appendix A). With this in hand, begin with the exegesis of Mark, beginning with chapter 1. First focus on the author, when the Gospel was written, and the author's purpose for writing. Discuss the historical and cultural context. In doing so, also discuss key people, places, and terms. Discuss John's purpose, as defined by the prophetic conversation between God and Jesus in Mark 1:1–4. Discuss the meaning of key terms such as the "Kingdom of God," "Fishers of Men,"[18] "Son of Man,"[19] and the "Good News."[20] And observe the use of connector words in a sentence (e.g., *and, but*). Review pages 125 and 271 of *Living by the Book* for the discussions on "The Laws of Structure" and "Figures of Speech" respectively. As homework assignments, the students should continue to study the first five chapters of Mark, keeping in mind key places, key people, key terms, and connector words.

Biblical Interpretation (Session 2)

Distribute the examples provided with this text of previous student exegetical interpretations of Isaiah 43:1–7 and 2 Corinthians 5:17–19 (appendix B). These can be distributed for the class to use as a reference when conducting an exegesis of a text. The *New Interpreter's Bible and Commentary* (twelve-volume set) is recommended as an excellent reference when conducting

---

[18] Mark 1:17 (KJV).
[19] Mark 2:10 (NIV).
[20] Mark 1:15 (NIV).

exegetical work. For homework, the students should continue to read in Mark and begin to apply the information discussed in class. They should be able to identify the meaning of key words. They should look for literary relationships, figures of speech, parables, and connector words, while continuing to bear in mind the cultural and historical context of that time.

Biblical Interpretation (Session 3)

Discuss the parable of the four soils, and the miracles Jesus performed in chapter 5. Discuss as a possible link (perhaps the author's intent) Jesus teaching on faith, then performing four miracles (calming the storm, healing the demoniac in the graveyard, healing the woman with the issue of blood, and raising a little girl from the dead).

Biblical Interpretation (Session 4)

Discuss the fourteen genres in the Bible as stated in *Living by the Book*, pages 224–26. After discussing each one briefly, begin to look at an Old Testament narrative and consult Mathewson in identifying the protagonist, the antagonist, and the foil. Pull out of the narrative the "meaning" of the story.

Biblical Interpretation (Session 5)

Divide the class into groups. Assign and then discuss the personalities of the main characters and their actions in the following narratives: Abigail in 1 Sam. 25: 1–25, David in 2 Sam. 11:1–27, and David and Goliath in1 Sam. 17:1–58. Identify the protagonist, the antagonist, and the foil. Again, pull out of the narratives the "meaning" of the story.

Biblical Interpretation (Session 6)

Begin discussing now the prophetic books. Consult *How to Read the Bible for all Its Worth* (Fee, Stuart 2003) concerning conducting an exegesis from different genres of the Bible. Also consult and discuss the exegesis of Isaiah 43:1–7.

Biblical Interpretation (Session 7)

Again, consulting Fee, begin studying the various contextual forms of the book of Psalms (e.g., laments, thanksgiving psalms, salvation psalms, hymns of praise). Divide the class into groups and assign a psalm from each contextual form to each group to perform an exegesis, using all of the class handouts and Fee. Allow time in class for the groups to work together.

Biblical Interpretation (Session 8)

Continue discussing the groups' exegetical work regarding the Psalms.

Biblical Interpretation (Session 9)

Looking at another gospel account, review the parable of the lost sheep, the parable of the lost coin, and the parable of the lost son in Luke 15. Discuss the reasons why each one was lost: (1) the sheep just wandered off, (2) the coin was lost at no fault of its own, and (3) the son left home as a result of his own choosing and out of selfishness. Discuss the actions of the father to the son, as well as our Heavenly Father to the lost. Then discuss who was "lost": the prodigal son, his brother, or both.

Biblical Interpretation (Session 10)

Review handouts, PowerPoint presentations, and previous class discussions in preparation for the student assessment. The review can be in the form of a game or open discussions.

Biblical Interpretation (Session 11)

An exam or student assessment should be given at this time to assess what the student has learned in this module. An example assessment and answer key are provided (appendix C). Students should also be allowed time in class to conduct an exegesis of a text. Students may bring extra resources to use in class in order to do their exegetical work.

Module 2: Homiletics

Homiletics (Session 1)

In this module, the class continues to do exegetical work but now with the mind-set of how to take what they have learned and transform it into a sermon. Demonstrate to the class how to build the bridge between biblical interpretation and homiletics by asking the questions of scripture suggested by Hendricks and Hendricks:

- Is there an example for me to follow?
- Is there a sin to avoid?
- Is there a promise to claim?
- Is there a prayer to repeat?
- Is there a command to obey?
- Is there a condition to meet?

- Is there a verse to memorize?
- Is there an error to mark?
- Is there a challenge to face?[21]

Discuss how we take our exegetical information and begin to construct a sermon. Discuss the definition of a sermon and what comes to their mind when they think of a sermon. Practice how to put the pieces of a sermon together by using one of the scriptures previously discussed in class and the information obtained from doing the exegesis.

Homiletics (Session 2)

Review again the exegetical paper regarding Isaiah 43:1–7. Begin to draw up some main points related to the text that could be presented if the students were to preach using this text. Ask the questions posed by Chapell:

- What does the text mean?
- How do I know what the text means?
- What concerns caused the text to be written?
- What do we share in common with those to (or about) whom the text was written and/ or the one by whom the text was written?
- How should people now respond to the truths of the text?
- What is the most effective way I can communicate the meaning of the text?[22]

Begin to form the introduction and some main points, with an emphasis on application and relating it to today's audience. Discuss the importance of a good introduction, one that grabs the attention of the audience at the very beginning. Again, as with any text, remember to always ask the questions:

- What does the text mean?
- How do I know what the text means?
- What concerns caused the text to be written?
- What do we share in common with those to (or about) whom the text was written and/ or the one by whom the text was written?
- How should people now respond to the truths of the text?
- What is the most effective way I can communicate the meaning of the text?

---

[21] Howard G. Hendricks and William D. Hendricks, *Living by the Book, the Art and Science of Reading the Bible* (Chicago: Moody, 2007) 224–26. Used by permission of Moody Publishers.

[22] Bryan Chapell, *Christ-Centered Preaching: Redeeming the Expository Sermon* (Grand Rapids, MI: Baker Academic, 2005), 104–5. Used by permission of Baker Academic.

Homiletics (Session 3)

Review the Foundations of Biblical Teaching PowerPoint (appendix D). Discuss Jesus's teaching on spiritual blindness (Mark chapter 8), then healing a man who was physically blind. Determine the fallen condition focus (FCF) and apply Chapell's questions as you relate the scripture to today's audience. Also, discuss the styles of various preachers and public speakers, and what does and does not appeal to the students.

Homiletics (Session 4)

Discuss the importance of a good introduction, one that gains the attention of the audience. Review the speech evaluation form (appendix E) so that the students will see how they will be evaluated on their sermons. Discuss delivery techniques, voice levels, the use of vocalized pauses (e.g., umm, uh), eye coordination, and distractions. These also will be discussed again, and in-depth, in the Public Speaking module (consult chapter 12 of *The Art of Public Speaking*). To determine the order in which they will preach, have the students choose a number out of a hat.

The students preach at the end of the course, and the sermons should be videotaped. At the end of the class, show each student a video of his or her sermon so that he or she can see how much he or she has grown and if there are still any areas that can be improved upon. Before each student preaches, hand out the Speech Evaluation Form. The entire class, along with the instructor, critiques each student according to the questions on the speech evaluation form. After each student preaches, the entire class gives oral and written feedback on the sermon. The class affirms what the speaker did great regarding the sermon's content and each student's delivery technique. Also, discuss what areas the student could either improve on or expand on should he or she preach the same sermon during a Sunday morning worship service.

Module 3: Public Speaking

Public Speaking (Session 1)

Begin this session with a discussion regarding a controversial topic. The topic can be political or spiritual in nature (e.g., homosexuality in the church, right to life), or something revolving around a current news event. After allowing time for much-heated debates, inform the class that the purpose for allowing these discussions is to introduce the next module for the course, which is public speaking. Begin to introduce the methods of public speaking, but go into greater detail during the next session. Inform the class that they will be conducting a debate as part of this session. Choose a hot topic, and then inform the students that one team will have to argue in favor of the topic, and the other team will have to argue against the topic.

Depending on the size of the class, at least two topics may be chosen, with teams arguing for and against each topic.

Public Speaking (Session 2)

Introduce the methods of persuasion and discuss the four patterns of persuasive speeches (consult chapters 15 and 16 of *The Art of Public Speaking*). Allow time in class to watch the movie *The Great Debaters*.

Public Speaking (Session 3)

Discuss the main event (the debate between Harvard University and Wiley College) and the details that led up to the event. Also, discuss the characteristics and personal experiences of the main characters in the movie and how these played out in their defining moments during the Harvard/Willey debate. Allow the teams time in class to discuss their plan of action. Advise the class to use various resources in supporting their position, not just Bible verses.

Public Speaking (Session 4)

Discuss the four patterns of persuasion speeches. Also, discuss the main characters in *The Great Debaters* and their persuasive skills. Allow time in class for the teams to meet. Remind the group again to vary their resources. The students should be required to not only use the Bible, but to bring in statistics, news articles, and other information found in their research that would support their positions.

Public Speaking (Session 5)

Focus this session on delivery techniques (consult chapter 12, "The Art of Public Speaking"). Discuss voice levels, vocalized pauses (e.g., um, uh), hand and body movements, and eye coordination. Distribute the speech evaluation form so that the students will know ahead of time how they will be assessed as they are giving their presentations. Allow time in class again for the teams to plan out their presentations, determine who will give the team's opening and closing remarks, etc. Choose an outside judge (one or three) to be the official judge(s) of the debates.

Public Speaking (Session 6)

The students should be ready to debate! The debates should be videotaped. After the final remarks are given, critique each team's presentation for both content and delivery. After the critique is given, the winners should be announced by the judges.

Module 4: Leadership

Leadership (Session 1)

Introduce the various styles of leadership as defined by the organization MindTools[23]:

- Transactional leadership
- Autocratic leadership
- Bureaucratic leadership
- Charismatic leadership
- Democratic/participative leadership
- Laissez-faire leadership
- Task-oriented leadership
- People-oriented leadership
- Servant leadership
- Transformational leadership

Discuss the pros and cons of each leadership style and situations where each style may be advantageous.

Leadership (Session 2)

Continue with the discussion regarding various leadership styles. Ask each student to identify his or her own leadership style. Then, divide the class into groups of two, and ask the students to discuss their own personal leadership styles with their partner. The students should provide feedback to each other regarding whether they agree or disagree with their partner's personal assessment of what his or her own leadership style is. The purpose of this exercise is for the students to hear firsthand how their leadership style is perceived by others and then be able to compare this perception to what they personally believe their own leadership style is. Have an open discussion regarding the results.

Leadership (Session 3)

Discuss in detail Maxwell's twenty-one indispensable qualities of a leader: character, charisma, commitment, communication, competence, courage, discernment, focus, generosity, initiative, listening, passion, positive attitude, problem solving, relationships, responsibility, security, self-discipline, servanthood, teachability, and vision.

---

[23] http://www.mindtools.com/pages/article/newLDR_84.htm. Used by permission of Mindtools.

Leadership (Session 4)

Using the handout "the Makings of an Effective Leader, Part 1 (appendix F), discuss the differences between a leader and a manager. Also, discuss the leadership call of Moses, Jeremiah, and Gideon, and how each one responded to the call.

Leadership (Session 5)

Continuing with "The Makings of an Effective Leader, Part 1" (appendix F), discuss the various phases of the leadership call and ask the students if they can identify what phase they are currently in. Using the handout "The Makings of an Effective Leader, Part 2" (appendix G), discuss the characteristics of an effective leader.

Review and Prep for Sermons (Session 1)

This time should be used to wrap up the discussion on leadership, review any of the topics discussed, and/or allow the students to ask questions regarding their sermons.

Sermons (Sessions 1–3)

The sermons are given at the end of all of the sessions. Depending on the size of the class and the length of time allotted for all of the previous sessions, this can take up to two to three weeks. Those who preach and participate in the exit interviews following the sermons are considered to have finished the course. Before each student preaches, distribute the Speech Evaluation Form (appendix E). Each of the students, along with the instructor, should critique each presenter. Instruct the students that they do not have to include their name on the evaluation sheet when evaluating their classmates unless they desire to do so. After each student preaches, the entire class gives oral and written feedback on his or her sermon. The class should affirm what each student did great regarding the sermon content and each student's delivery technique. Also discuss what areas the student could either improve on or expand on should he or she preach the same sermon during a Sunday morning worship service. All of the completed speech evaluation forms should be handed to each student after he or she preaches.

Evaluation and Feedback (Sessions 1–3)

Conduct exit interviews with each student. For ease of facilitation, exit interview questions are provided in appendix H. During the exit interviews, each student should be shown a video of his or her own sermon and debate presentations. This is done so that the student can see how much he or she has grown spiritually. Discuss with the students any areas needing improvement, particularly with regard to their public speaking skills and sermon/lesson preparation.

After all of the sermons are given, and the exit interviews are completed, the class is officially over.

BIBLIOGRAPHY

Chapell, Bryan. *Christ-Centered Preaching: Redeeming the Expository Sermon.* Grand Rapids, MI: Baker Academic, 2005.

Fee, Gordon and Douglas Stuart. *How to Read the Bible for All Its Worth.* Grand Rapids, MI: Zondervan, 2003.

Hendricks, Howard G. and William D. *Living by the Book: The Art and Science of Reading the Bible.* Chicago: Moody Publishers, 2007.

Lucas, Stephen E. *The Art of Public Speaking.* New York: McGraw-Hill, 2009.

———. *The Art of Public Speaking, Instructor's Manual.* New York: McGraw-Hill, 2009.

Maxwell, John C. *The 21 Indispensable Qualities of a Leader: Becoming the Person Others Want to Follow.* Nashville: Thomas Nelson, 1999.

Mindtools. "Leadership Styles." Accessed June 5, 2016 http://www.mindtools.com/pages/article/newLDR_84.htm

Warren, Rick. *The Purpose Driven Life.* Grand Rapids, MI: Zondervan, 2002.

APPENDIX A

Principles of Biblical Interpretation

An Inductive Study Method

The Role of the Biblical Expositor

- The biblical expositor is an interpreter and a communicator. His/her task is to interpret God's Word and to communicate this interpretation to his or her audience, upon which their eternal destiny hangs.
- "Do your best to present yourself to God as one approved, a workman who does not need to be ashamed and who correctly handles the word of truth"

  2 Timothy 2:15 (NIV)

The Importance of Good Biblical Exposition

– Biblical interpretation is transformative. It provides a deeper and more thorough understanding of God's word, and thus deepens our relationship with Him.

– Biblical interpretation provides the foundation for our own personal spiritual and theological development, as well as our own biblical worldview.

– Having an accurate understanding of God's word, based upon a thorough exegesis of the text, prevents us from believing in false teaching.

The Importance of Good Biblical Exposition (cont'd)

– Grammatical and Literary Analysis allows us to understand the text intellectually, based on our finite wisdom and understanding. Historical Analysis helps us to understand the "story behind the text", the "story of the text" and the "story in front of the text".

– Our faith, in conjunction with the help of the Holy Spirit, allows us to understand the text spiritually.

– "I pray that the eyes of your heart may be enlightened in order that you may know the hope to which he has called you, the riches of his glorious inheritance in his holy people, and his incomparably great power for us who believe…" Ephesians 1: 17-19 (NIV)

Principles and Methods of Interpretation

❑First, be suspicious of the text, a scriptural profiler! Observation is key.

❑Always keep in mind the story behind the text, the story of the text, and the story in front of the text.

❑Become familiar with the cultural context at that time, the "sitz en laben" – the context in which the text was written.

❑Don't forget to ask the question – "how does this relate to me?"

Principles and Methods of Interpretation

❑Ask the five interrogative questions: who, what, when, where, and why. Who is writing, and to whom is he writing to? What is the message? When was it written? Where was the author at the time the passage was written? And why was it written, for what purpose?

❑Become saturated with the particulars of the passage – the historical, cultural, and literary contexts.

Principles and Methods of Interpretation

❑Historical-Critical Method of Analysis- become familiar with the historical context (date the text was written, where it was written, to whom it was written, political and religious leaders of that time period, current events (i.e. Passover, Feast of Unleavened Bread, Census).

❑Look for key places and the relevance of each

❑Become "one" with the Author! Research the life of the author, the author's style of writing, beliefs and opinions of the author

Principles and Methods of Interpretation

❑Cultural Contextual Method of Analysis - Become familiar with the cultural context at that time

❑"Sitz en laben" – the current context (what was happening) during the time in which the text was written.

❑Analyze key words/terms/phrases and key people as they relate to both the historical and cultural context of the text.

Principles and Methods of Interpretation

❑Literary Contextual Method of Analysis – Learn the literary genre of the text (i.e. narrative, prophecy, parable, poetry)

❑Look for figures of speech (e.g. metaphors, similes, allegories)

❑Look for common themes as you become familiar with the broader context of the passage (the verse within the Chapter/Book/Old and New Testament/Bible)

Principles and Methods of Interpretation

- Prayer and observation are key!

- Remember to ask the five interrogative questions: who, what, when, where, and why. Who is writing, and to whom is he writing to? What is the message? When was it written? Where was the author at the time the passage was written? And why was it written, for what purpose?
- Relate what you have learned to today's audience. What is this text saying to me?

- Invest in biblical study tools

APPENDIX B

Student Exegetical Interpretations

Isaiah 43:1–7 and 2 Corinthians 5:17–19

Isaiah 43:1–7

An Exegesis

In this passage, we see God as Israel's creator, precious promises to Israel of His presence with them in their affliction, and their deliverance out of captivity. We see that despite the Israelites' spiritual failure, God said that He would still show them mercy, that He would bring them back from captivity, and that He would restore them. He would give them an outpouring of love, not wrath. Then the world would know that God alone had done this. Yahweh promised to bring back together His "unworthy" servants for His glory; therefore, they should not fear. The theme in this passage is that Yahweh is the source of salvation and deliverance for the nation of Israel and for the people of God.

Historical Context

The book of Isaiah is a collection of prophetic oracles and sayings by the prophet Isaiah. There is much debate over the authorship of the book of Isaiah. For the most part it is agreed by scholars that the book was written by at least two different authors. The first thirty-nine chapters are indictment and judgment oracles. These are accredited to Isaiah Ben Amoz, and these chapters are often referred to as the first book of Isaiah. Micah and Isaiah are the first known classical prophets of the Southern Kingdom. Preclassical prophets announced God's plans for the king of that time. Classical prophets announced God's plans for His people. Isaiah lived in eighth century BC. Prophets not only spoke for God, but they also spoke out against social injustices and political leaders in their day. The audiences were the people of God. Biblical prophets appeared during times of trouble.

During the second half of the eighth century, the Neo-Assyrian Empire was taking its place as the first world power known in history. Isaiah was a prophet during the time when the original nation of Israel had been divided into two kingdoms—Israel in the north and Judah in the south. Both kingdoms had sinned greatly against God. They perverted justice, oppressed the poor, and sought help from neighboring pagan nations instead of turning to God for guidance and direction in time of need. Isaiah came primarily as a prophet to Judah, but his message was also for the Northern Kingdom. Two major events are the focus of chapters 1–39: the invasion of Israel by the Assyrian king, King Tiglath-Pileser III; and the invasion of Judah by the Assyrian king, King Sennacherib, in 701. Isaiah brings a message of divine judgment for both Israel and Judah. Through the prophet Isaiah, God foretells of the destruction of Assyria and other evil surrounding nations.

Beginning in chapter 40, there is a major shift in writing style and tone. The author is more poetic and theoretical, and the tone is more conciliatory in nature. The people being addressed are in exile rather than in eighth century Judah. These chapters are referred to as Second Isaiah, and to some, Second and Third Isaiah. Isaiah is divided into three books: chapters 1–35 refer to God's anger and mercy; chapters 36–39 make reference to God's delivering power, and chapters 40–66 refer to God's benevolent plans and purposes. In book one, Yahweh will bring judgment upon Judah and the world for their unrighteousness, but will also later bring about the blessings of the kingdom of Israel. In book two, Babylon is the background. Yahweh is the source of salvation and deliverance for the nation of Israel. In book three, the message is one of the "Suffering Servant," redemption, and the return of the Messiah. Reminiscent of His promise to the exiles coming out of Egypt, God assures Israel of His personal presence. Use of the words *water* and *rivers* could also refer to Israel's victory at the Red Sea. *Fire* can give reference to the "iron furnace" of Egypt's oppression and slavery, or to the siege of Jerusalem in the previous chapter, or to the fiery furnace of the Hebrew boys. Fire also can be interpreted as an instrument of testing and refining us as we see in Psalm 66 and in Malachi.

Legal terminology is applied to the mighty acts of God in verse 3. First, as a kinsman redeemer, we see God redeemed His people. He protected them as their kinsman in law. Verses three and four represent the Savior arranging a legal transaction by which Cyrus is to get Egypt, with Ethiopia and Seba to the south thrown in, in exchange for Israel's freedom. Historically we find that it was actually not Cyrus but his son, Camyses, who conquered Egypt in 525 BC. In verse 3, Isaiah is giving Israel an understanding of how much it means to God. Egypt and the adjoining countries were regarded as exceptionally wealthy, so the fact that these are named as Israel's ransom attests to the high value placed upon it by the Lord. To the Lord, Israel was worth more than the rest of humanity put together. Certainly, this is the meaning when God goes on to say, "You are precious in thy sight." No price of ransom is too high for members of His family.

We are first introduced to the concept of "kinsman redeemer" in the book of Ruth. Vine's dictionary defines the word *redeem* as "to buy out, especially, in the purchasing of a slave with a view to his freedom." It also means "to release in receipt of ransom." In the New Testament, we see the redemptive work of Jesus Christ, bringing deliverance through His death, from the guilt and power of sin. He paid the ultimate sacrifice that we all, Jew and Gentile, may have eternal life.

Verses 5 through 7 are further proof of God's loving relationship with His children, with the promise of redemption including a family reunion. Due to a worldwide dispersal of its people, Israel had lost its identity as a nation. But now God will fulfill His promise and bring His family home from the east, west, north, and south, every corner of the earth. Israel was to be a witness and promote the divine glory by the visible illustration of its deliverance.

The author was speaking primarily of Israel's return from Babylon. But there is a broader meaning, which is that all of God's children will be regathered when Christ comes to rule in His place over the earth. The ingathering of the exiles is a favorite theme of "Deutero-Isaiah," also found in chapter 49.

Synthesis and Conclusion

Isaiah is remembered for his magnificent conception of God. Isaiah knew that God is holy. Early in his book, in chapter 6, verse 3 (NIV), we read the words "Holy, holy, holy is the Lord

Almighty; the whole earth is full of His glory." The title "Holy One of Israel" was used almost exclusively by Isaiah in the Old Testament. The concept of holiness was not unique to Israel. To Israel, the holiness of God indicated His perfection, His purity, and His Supreme Being above all other gods. Yahweh is Lord of all, King of the Universe, the Lord of history who exhibits His character and righteousness. In addition to Isaiah's emphasis on God's holiness, there is the overall concern for obedience to God. Isaiah knew that sin was rebellion against the Lord, and he knew that only God could forgive sin. In chapter 43, we see the promise of deliverance. We can even go beyond that to see the awesome redemptive work of Jesus Christ, and the free gift of salvation through His grace. We see an example of God's love as a Heavenly Father. We see His promises to those who are His. For His children, no price is too high. And, for His children no situation is too great that He can't handle it.

Reflections

The book of Isaiah has several messages, two of which are redemption and the return of the Messiah. The eschatology found in the book of Isaiah is a kingdom eschatology. The emphasis is on the future kingdom of Israel. It is seen as a kingdom centered in Jerusalem, where there is true worship, and Yahweh reigns as King. Isaiah stressed the "Day of Yahweh, a time when the presence of God would be readily discoverable in human history."

Isaiah also demanded social and religious righteousness practiced in humility and faith. Isaiah reminds all of us who are called to the ministry to be dutiful in the call, to continue to stand for God's word and on God's word.

Exegesis of a Pauline Passage

I. Establish the text.

   A. Pericope: 2 Corinthians 5:17–19.

   B. This pericope within the letter. Paul wrote 2 Corinthians to affirm his ministry, to defend his authority, and to renounce false teachers who had come to the church at Corinth challenging Paul's integrity, his authority, and his ministry. After Paul wrote 1 Corinthians, his second letter to the church at Corinth, he continued his ministry at Ephesus until he heard that his second letter had not completely accomplished what he had hoped it would; that is, unity within the Corinthian church. First Corinthians was written to address issues in the church involving division and disorder, Christian marriage, Christian religion, public worship, and the resurrection. Paul continues to deal with issues in the church related to parties or cliques, immorality, basic power issues, marginalization of some people, and doubts concerning his authority and integrity. Timothy had arrived in Corinth and found the church still having internal disputes and now being suspicious of Paul. Paul's authority as an apostle and his integrity were being challenged. Therefore, Paul writes 2 Corinthians to defend his position and to denounce those who were twisting the truth.

     This pericope deals with his love for Christ and his commitment to leading others in right fellowship with God, just as God through Christ reconciled him (Paul) back to Himself. In the first nine chapters, Paul addresses his own sincerity and integrity, and he affirms his relationship with the Corinthians, his authority in Christ, and his apostolic ministry of reconciliation and being in right fellowship with God and man. Paul is restating his ministry to demonstrate the validity of his message, the sincerity of his heart, his love for Christ, and to urge them not to listen to the false doctrine being taught.

   C. This pericope within the form of a letter. This pericope is located in the body of the letter. It is located in the fourth letter to the Corinthian church. It is part of an ongoing dialogue or relationship between Paul and the church at Corinth. It is written in the style of an apologetic.

   D. This pericope within its setting. Paul begins 2 Corinthians with an opening address and thanksgiving for the God of all comfort. He tells them of the hardships that he had faced. He does not give them specific details but does say, "This happened that we might not rely on ourselves but on God who raises the dead" (1:9, NIV). Paul further explains his actions, his reasons for postponing his visit, a report of the ministry from Troas, and then goes on to defend his apostolic ministry and, basically, the Gospel. His openness and honesty with them was a demonstration to them of the purity of his heart, that there was no pretense concerning him and his love for them.

     Paul gives a teaching on the resurrection, since there were questions still regarding this, and then goes straight into false prophets. Paul goes on to talk about those who take pride in what is seen rather than what is in the heart. These were the false teachers who were only concerned with money and popularity. Paul, on the other hand, is telling them that there is nothing false or hidden concerning him or his ministry— that it is "plain to God," and he hopes it is also "plain to your conscience" (5:11, NIV). While the false preachers were preaching for fame and money, Paul and his companions were preaching for the sake of eternal life, for right relationships between God and men. This is the driving point of this pericope in the text. Everything that Paul and his companions did was to honor God, and not themselves. Christ's love controlled their lives. He says in the verse right before it, "so from now on we regard no one from a worldly point of view. Though we once regarded Christ in this way, we do so no longer" (5:16, NIV). This indicates that there has been a change, or rather a transformation, in his heart. Something had taken place to give him this change of heart. Paul begins in verse 17 to say that those who are in Christ are brand new creations and that because God brings us back to Himself, we in turn have the privilege of encouraging others to do the same, and thus we are those who have the ministry of reconciliation. Right after the verse, he reminds them that we are Christ's ambassadors. We represent Christ, and therefore we have the responsibility of leading others to reconciliation with God. On Christ's behalf, we are to implore people to be reconciled to God. Paul opens his heart, states that there is nothing false concerning him or his ministry, states his ministry, and then charges others to join him in the ministry of reconciliation. Here also he is stating his theology, and he is reminding them of who gives him the authority.

E. Sentence structure. The first part of the sentence states, "Therefore if anyone is in Christ, he is a new creation." (2 Corinthians 5:17, ESV) In other words, those who are in Christ are defined as "new creations." The two are one and the same. The second part breaks down what is meant by being "in Christ." There is a pause with the semicolon, after which comes further explanation. "The old has passed away;" (pause), then "behold, the new has come!" The break in this sentence by the comma indicates the opposites on either side of the comma (the old versus the new). The ministry of reconciliation is defined after the semicolon in the following verse (verse 19).

F. English translation. RSV says "creation" or "creature." The New Revised Standard Version reads, "So if anyone is in Christ, there is a new creation: everything old has passed away, see, everything has become new!" It is indicated in the commentaries that in the Greek this verse may mean by the power and act of God, a new creation.

II. Key words.

A. The key words in this pericope are: *old, new, creation, reconciliation, God, Christ, in Christ.*
B. Meaning of the words:
   1. *Old*—referring to a previous life, one which could be described as having a worldly view. From Paul's perspective, in this verse *old* refers to a life not indicative of a

"conversion" or "experience" with Christ. One which is still centered in the flesh, in idolatry and immorality as much of the Greco-Roman world was at that time.

2. *New*—referring to an inner change, a transformation. A new life in Christ, according to Paul, would be indicative of one that had an undying love for Christ and his/her fellow man.

3. *Creation*—Creation in this sense means "being," not in the physical sense but in the spiritual sense.

4. *God*—Our Heavenly Father, who loved us so much that He reconciled us back to Him through His Son, Jesus Christ.

5. *Christ*—Our Redeemer, the One through which we have fellowship with our Heavenly Father. Through redemption we have been restored for the fulfillment of God's purposes in us.

6. *Reconciliation*—to restore to friendship, to right relationship, to fellowship.

7. *In Christ*—Being united with Christ, living in union with Christ, and therefore being one with the Father.

C. The English translation—2 Corinthians 5:17–19 (ESV)—"Therefore, if anyone is in Christ, he is a new creation. The old has passed away; behold, the new has come. All this is from God, who through Christ reconciled us to himself and gave us the ministry of reconciliation; that is, in Christ God was reconciling the world to himself, not counting their trespasses against them, and entrusting to us the message of reconciliation."

D. Logic of the pericope: Paul is defending his ministry and the authority that he has in Christ. Being in Christ is an indication that the new creation, the reversal of the sinful nature, is now in process; the old way of looking at things from a human perspective has passed away and no longer has validity. As a result of Christ undoing the damage that was caused by the fall of man, trespasses are canceled. And human beings are reconciled to God. Paul presents basically the free gift of salvation, what men have received from Christ who died for their sake and was raised. We are now united with Christ through faith in Him and commitment to Him. The capacity to see both our fellow men and Christ in their true light comes from this inner transformation wrought by being in Christ. This redemptive work that Christ has done to help and transform men is from God. God did it all through Christ, who reconciled us unto Himself. The word reconcile reminds us that God not only removed the guilt or penalty of sin but brought about restored personal relationship with Him, between Himself and His redeemed people. Just as the Gospel is for everyone, Paul was also for everyone. His message was inclusive, not exclusive. He took joy in being an ambassador for Christ, and therefore leading others into right relationship with God just as he was restored. Paul includes this message in the letter because he is not only defending his own authority but also the Gospel against those who were teaching false doctrine.

III. Establish the historical context.

A. Who is the audience: Paul was writing to the Corinthian church, particularly to the Hellenistic Jewish Christians who had come into the church and who were challenging his authority and integrity. They were Hellenistic Jewish Christian missionaries who were competing for the affection, loyalty, and support of the Corinthian church. They claimed to be servants of Christ (2 Corinthians 11:23). They had glowing reviews of their preaching elsewhere (2 Corinthians 3:1). They were attacking Paul by saying that his preaching was ineffective, and that while his letters were impressive, in person he was weak and lacking in his ability to preach. Paul makes a quick visit to the church, only to be attacked and humiliated publicly (2 Corinthians 2:5–8; 7:12). He leaves and then writes his third letter.

B. Why is Paul writing? Paul is writing because his ministry and integrity had been challenged by false teachers coming into the church at Corinth.

C. When is Paul writing? Paul wrote 2 Corinthians around 55 CE, near the end of his three-year ministry in Ephesus.

D. From where is Paul writing? Paul wrote the letter from Macedonia.

E. The relationship between Paul and the letter's recipients. Paul established the church at Corinth on his second missionary journey. In the beginning, Paul's preaching was enthusiastically received by the Corinthians. However, due to outside influences, the church had deteriorated. Some were still supportive of Paul. Others were confused due to the false teaching that had begun to take place.

IV. The pericope within context.

A. Paul's basic affirmation. Paul affirms what Christ did on the cross for us, so that we would be one with Him. Paul is not only stating the Gospel message, but he is also, I believe, speaking from his "experience" or his "encounter" with God. Paul's view of the world and Christ changed from that point on. As he points out in the scripture, he no longer regards anyone, even Christ, from a worldly view (2 Corinthians 5:16).

B. Paul's basic affirmation within the Pauline context. Paul is stating in this pericope his theological stance. Another similar scripture in the Pauline corpus can be found in Romans 5:10–11 (NIV), which reads, "For if, when we were God's enemies, we were reconciled to him through the death of his Son, how much more, having been reconciled, shall we be saved through his life! Not only is this so, but we also rejoice in God through our Lord Jesus Christ, through whom we have now received reconciliation." Also, in Galatians 6:15 (NIV) he writes, "Neither circumcision nor uncircumcision means anything; what counts is a new creation." In other words, Paul was reiterating his belief that you did not have to be a Jew to be saved. What matters is the inner transformation, which can only take place through Christ, by the power of God.

C. Paul's basic affirmation within the New Testament context. Paul affirms John 3:16 (KJV), "For God so loved the world that He gave His only begotten Son, that whosoever believeth in Him should not perish, but have everlasting life". Again, God showing His love toward us, and pours out His grace, His mercy, and His unconditional love toward us through His Son, that we might enjoy fellowship with Him.

D. Paul's basic affirmation within the Biblical context. Paul begins his theological stance from the beginning with Adam and Eve and their fall in the Garden of Eden (Genesis 3). However, he then takes us to the point of the free gift of salvation, to Christ who died for our sins (1 Corinthians 15:3). Paul takes us from under the law, to grace and to love, which is the fulfillment of the law (Romans 13:10).

E. Paul's basic affirmation within the Christian context. Paul affirms the basic Christian theological perspective that Jesus came to set the captives free (Luke 4:18–19, Isaiah 61:1–2): free from the penalty of sin, free in order that we may spend eternal life with Him. Paul also makes clear that it is by the power of God. It is not something that we can do ourselves. This is a very important point in preaching liberation theology. In liberation theology Jesus is not only looked upon as our Savior, but also as our Deliverer, as the One who can perform miracles and do the impossible. He is the One who can deliver us from injustices, from sickness, from addictions, from situations where we have no control and can't see our way out.

V. Paul's affirmation(s) and your church.

A. My paraphrase of the Pauline message. God loves me, and He desires a relationship with me. So much so that He sent His Son that I may accept Him, and therefore enjoy fellowship with my Heavenly Father. Also, because God has done this for me, it is now my responsibility to tell others such that they may have and enjoy the same relationship that I have with my Heavenly Father.

B. The situation in your church. I have recently had to deal with a young woman who was abused by her husband. During this abusive marriage, she had an affair. What I explained to her was that God had already forgiven her and that He loves her. Too many times we carry around the weight of our sins, forgetting that Christ already paid it all for us. I believe too many of us never live our full potential because we have yet to take hold of the revelation that God loves us. We say that we accept Him as our personal Lord and Savior. But it is hard for us to grasp the fact that the God who created heaven and earth loves us! And in addition, He loves us unconditionally!

C. Paul's message in your church. This pericope spoke to my heart because I can see how God has changed my heart. I believe this pericope is fitting not only at the point of salvation, but also as we grow closer in our walk with him. As we are in the sanctification process, we are continuing to shed our old desires, and those things that once appealed to us don't appeal to us anymore in the same fashion. I would teach this from the standpoint that God does a work on the inside of us. He digs up and digs out those things that are not of Him, that He may perform a great work in us and through us, and because He is continually making us like Him. When I also think of those things that we shed as we are being transformed on the inside, I think of an onion. You can visualize pealing an onion. That is what I feel like when God is getting rid of "stuff" in our lives and in our hearts. The change may not be noticeable on the outside, but the layers have come off on the inside. God's love is a profound message to teach. And one that is so needed.

My goal is to have a shelter for abused women and their children. What I would share with them from this point is that God loves them and that they can begin again. I don't know quite how to answer why it happened. I know enough to be able to tell them that they did nothing to deserve it, that Christ loves them, that they can live a joyous life, and that, at some point, they will be able to get beyond the hurt and suffering, and live again.

VI. Reader criticism. I bring my own circumstances of having been hurt by life's experiences, which also include being treated a certain way based on gender and race. Having said that, this pericope brings comfort and joy to me. Just knowing that God loves me, that's enough right there. I don't think we can bring that message home enough. In addition, just the fact that God desires a relationship with us is astounding!

APPENDIX C

Biblical Interpretation Assessment

Introduction to Biblical Interpretation

Name: _____ Date: _____

Please circle the correct answer.

1. Each truth of a text of Scripture:
    a) Must be confirmed by a commentary
    b) Must be validated by a qualified teacher
    c) Will never change
    d) None of the above

2. The words *but, however,* or *nevertheless* are often used to show:
    a) Continuity
    b) Contrast
    c) Comparison
    d) None of the above

3. Which of these is not a type of biblical literature:
    a) Prophetic
    b) Biographical
    c) Romance
    d) Historical

4. The three parts of inductive study are:
    a) Observation, interpretation, application
    b) Looking, seeing, understanding
    c) Observation, interpretation, commitment
    d) None of the above

5. Key words are:
    a) People, places, or events
    b) Words that summarize the text
    c) Words that are vital to understanding the text
    d) a and c

6. The 5 *W*'s and *H* are:
    a) Questions Jesus answered in Matthew
    b) Not crucial to understanding the Bible
    c) Each book is a complete book in itself
    d) Asked when getting the details of the text

7. You should study the Bible one book at a time because:
   a) There is too much material otherwise
   b) Each book was written by a different author
   c) Each book is a complete message within itself
   d) It would take too long to study the whole Bible

8. Words such as *therefore, for, so that*, and *for this reason* indicate:
   a) comparison
   b) sequence of events
   c) explanation
   d) contrast

9. Which of the following is not something the overview of the book helps with:
   a) seeing the entire message of the book
   b) identifying the author
   c) becoming aware of the structure of the book
   d) identifying the main theme of the book

10. To discover the context of a passage you must first:
    a) study the text objectively
    b) study the text subjectively
    c) read the passage devotionally
    d) none of the above

11. The ultimate goal of personal Bible study is:
    a) A transformed life and deep relationship with Christ
    b) To preach successfully
    c) To understand your pastor's sermons

12. When you observe the text, you should begin by:
    a) asking the 5W's and H
    b) looking for things that are obvious
    c) reading the entire book in which the text is found
    d) determining how the text applies to your own life

13. A topical study is:
    a) list of key words
    b) list of topics you are interested in learning from the text
    c) a list of topics occurring within the text
    d) a topical study where you investigate all Scriptural passages dealing with that topic

14. (True or false) The book of Revelation falls under the apocalyptic genre.

15. (True or false) Inductive study is a learning process that cannot be learned overnight.

16. (True or false) An overview enables you to discover the overall context of an author's message.

17. (True or false) God is the ultimate author of Scripture.

18. (True or false) The word *context* means, "That which goes against the text."

19. (True or false) If you try to look for the obscure things, you will automatically pick up the obvious things.

20. (True or false) In writing a paragraph summary, you should use as few words as possible.

21. (True or false) Inductive study uses the Bible as the primary source of information.

22. (True or false) The basis for accurate observation is careful interpretation.

23. (True or false) The key verse is a verse that best expresses the theme of the chapter.

24. (True or false) Your paragraph theme should be chosen in light of the chapter theme.

25. (True or false) In an inductive study, you should consult commentaries when you fail to understand the text.

Exegetical Exercise

Introduction to Biblical Interpretation

Answer Key

Name: _____ Date: _____

Please circle the correct answer.

1. Each truth of a text of Scripture:
    a) Must be confirmed by a commentary
    b) Must be validated by a qualified teacher
    c) **Will never change**
    d) None of the above

2. The words *but, however,* or *nevertheless* are often used to show:
    a) Continuity
    b) **Contrast**
    c) Comparison
    d) None of the above

3. Which of these is not a type of biblical literature:
    a) Prophetic
    b) Biographical
    c) **Romance**
    d) Historical

4. The three parts of Inductive Study are:
    a) **Observation, interpretation, application**
    b) Looking, seeing, understanding
    c) Observation, interpretation, commitment
    d) None of the above

5. Key words are:
    a) People, places, or events
    b) Words which summarize the text
    c) Words which are vital to understanding the text
    d) **a and c**

6. The 5 *W*'s and *H* are:
    a) Questions Jesus answered in Matthew
    b) Not crucial to understanding the Bible
    c) Each book is a complete book in itself
    d) **Asked when getting the details of the text**

7. You should study the Bible one book at a time because:
   a) **There is too much material otherwise**
   b) Each book was written by a different author
   c) Each book is a complete message within itself
   d) It would take too long to study the whole Bible

8. Words such as *therefore*, *for*, *so that*, and *for this reason* indicate:
   a) comparison
   b) sequence of events
   c) **explanation**
   d) contrast

9. Which of the following does the overview of the book help with?
   a) seeing the entire message of the book
   b) identifying the author
   c) identifying the main theme of the book
   d) **all of the above**

10. To discover the context of a passage you must first:
    a) study the text objectively
    b) study the text subjectively
    c) **read the passage devotionally**
    d) none of the above

11. The ultimate goal of personal Bible study is:
    a) **A transformed life and deep relationship with Christ**
    b) To preach successfully
    c) To understand your pastor's sermons

12. When you observe the text, you should begin by:
    a) asking the 5*W*'s and *H*
    b) **looking for things that are obvious**
    c) reading the entire book in which the text is found
    d) determining how the text applies to your own life

13. A topical study is:
    a) list of key words
    b) list of topics you are interested in learning from the text
    c) a list of topics occurring within the text
    d) **a topical study where you investigate all Scriptural passages dealing with that topic**

14. (**True** or false) The book of Revelation falls under the Apocalyptic genre.

15. (**True** or false) Inductive study is a learning process that cannot be learned overnight.

16. (**True** or false) An overview enables you to discover the overall context of an author's message.

17. (**True** or false) God is the ultimate author of Scripture.

18. (True or **false**) The word *context* means, "That which goes against the text."

19. (**True** or false) If you try to look for the obscure things, you will automatically pick up the obvious things.

20. (**True** or false) In writing a paragraph summary, you should use as few words as possible.

21. (**True** or false) Inductive study uses the Bible as the primary source of information.

22. (**True** or false) The basis for accurate observation is careful interpretation.

23. (**True** or false) The key verse is a verse that best expresses the theme of the chapter.

24. (**True** or false) Your paragraph theme should be chosen in light of the chapter theme.

25. (**True** or false) In conducting an inductive study, you should consult commentaries when you fail to understand the text.

Exegetical Exercise

APPENDIX D

Foundations of Biblical Preaching

Focusing On The Process

Focusing On The Process

- What is a sermon?

  "A sermon is a statement of faith drawn from the text of the tradition and projecting the authentic being of the preacher. A sermon is not a lecture but a work of art."*

* James M. Wall, "The Sermon: A Work of Art", the Christian Ministry7/6, Nov., 1976:28

Focusing On The Process

❑ Why Preach?

Romans 10:14-15 (NIV)– "How then can they call on the one they have not believed in? And how can they believe in the one of whom they have not heard? And how can they hear without someone preaching to them? And how can they preach unless they are sent. As it is written, "How beautiful are the feet of those who bring good news!"

❑ Our authority – The Word Of God

Focusing on The Process

❑ What is expository preaching?

- "An expository message is one whose structure and thought are derived from a biblical text, that covers the scope of the text, and that explains the features and context of the text in order to disclose the enduring principles for faithful thinking, living, and worship intended by the Spirit, who inspired the text".*

- "The goal of expository preaching is to show how God's Word discloses His will for those united with Him through His Son."*

* B. Chapell, Christ-Centered Preaching, Redeeming the Expository Sermon, 2nd Edition (Grand Rapids: Baker Academic, 2005) 31

Focusing On The Process

❑ The goal of the preacher:

» "To approach the task with a deep sense of dependence on the Spirit of God."*

» To prepare. Preparation is key. It doesn't come by osmosis!

» To remember that "popular acclaim is not necessarily the same as spiritual effectiveness".*

» To remember that the "technical excellence of a message may rest on your skills, but the Spiritual efficacy of the message rests with God".*

* B. Chapell, Christ-Centered Preaching, Redeeming the Expository Sermon, 2nd Edition (Grand Rapids: Baker Academic, 2005) 33

Focusing On The Process

❑ The Fallen Condition Focus (FCF)

"The mutual human condition that contemporary believers share with those to or about whom the text was written that requires the grace of the passage for God's people to glorify and enjoy Him"*

*B. Chapell, Christ-Centered Preaching, Redeeming the Expository Sermon, 2nd Edition (Grand Rapids: Baker Academic, 2005) 50

Focusing On The Process

- "The purpose of the sermon must be evident in the passage:

  - What does the text say?

  - What spiritual concern(s) did the text address (in its context)?

  - What spiritual concerns do listeners share in common with those to (or about) whom the text is written?"*

*B. Chapell, Christ-Centered Preaching, Redeeming the Expository Sermon, 2nd Edition (Grand Rapids: Baker Academic, 2005) 52

Focusing On The Process

- The Need for Application

  - And you say that to say what?

  - "Textual information (pre-sermon material) + addressing a textually rooted FCF + relevant textual application = sermon (sermonic message)."*

  - Without application "the congregation may be left without any true insights as to what the passage is really about and without having received any clear teaching about God or themselves".*

*B. Chapell, Christ-Centered Preaching, Redeeming the Expository Sermon, 2nd Edition (Grand Rapids: Baker Academic, 2005) 56, 55, 54

Focusing On The Process

❑ When choosing a text, keep in mind the following: 1) your personal level of experience in biblical interpretation; the culture, and to the extent possible, the background of the audience; the event or occasion itself; and the time allowed for the sermonic message.

• "An expository unit is a large or a small portion of Scripture from which a preacher can demonstrate a single spiritual truth with adequate supporting facts or concepts arising within the scope of the text."* (i.e., The Prodigal Son)

*B. Chapell, Christ-Centered Preaching, Redeeming the Expository Sermon, 2nd Edition (Grand Rapids: Baker Academic, 2005) 61

Focusing On The Process

- Select passages that are of a particular interest to you (Be careful not to impose your views on the text). The message must first speak to the messenger!

- Sermon topics should include those that speak to the needs of the audience.

- Stories (real or fictional) are great ways to introduce a message or to emphasize a message.

- Allow the Holy Spirit to guide you

Focusing On The Process

- Methods for Biblical Interpretation

    - Grammatical Historical Method
    - Using grammar and history to discern a text's original meaning
    - Observe the Historical, Cultural, and Literary Context
    - Determine the redemptive context (How does this passage function in the entire pericope or Scripture?)

Focusing On The Process

❑ Invest in Biblical Study Tools

- ▪ Various Interpretations
- ▪ Biblical Concordance
- ▪ Lexicons
- ▪ Bible Dictionaries, Encyclopedias, Handbooks

APPENDIX E

Speech Evaluation Form

Speech Evaluation Form

SPEAKER _____

TOPIC_____

Rate the speaker on each point: E-Excellent; G-Good; A-Average; F-Fair; P-Poor

ACTIVITY	E	G	A	F	P
INTRODUCTION					
Gained attention and interest					
Introduced topic clearly					
Related topic to audience					
Established credibility					
Previewed body of speech					
DELIVERY					
Began speech w/o rushing					
Maintained strong eye contact					
Avoided distracting mannerisms					
Articulated words clearly					
Used pauses effectively					
Used vocal variety to add impact					
Presented visual aids well					
Communicated enthusiam for topic					
Departed from lectern w/o rushing					
BODY					
Main points clear					
Main points fully supported					
Organization well planned					
Language accurate					
Language clear					
Language appropriate					
Connectives effective					

CONCLUSION					
Prepare audience for ending					
Reinforced central idea					
Vivid ending					
OVERALL EVALUATION					
Met assignment					
Topic challenging					
Specific purpose well chosen					
Message adapted to audience					
Speech completed w/in time limit					
Held interest of audience					

What did the speaker do most effectively?

What should the speaker pay special attention to next time?

General Comments

APPENDIX F

The Makings of an Effective Leader, Part 1

Connie Welch Ministries
Emmanuel Christian Institute

Part 1—Leadership Seminar—"The Makings of an Effective Leader"

I. Definition of the term leader—A leader leads by guidance, by direction, or by example:

   a. A person who leads or commands a group, organization, or country.[24]
   b. A person followed by others.
   c. "A person who leads: as a: guide, conductor b (1): a person who directs a military force or unit (2): a person who has commanding authority or influence."[25]
   d. A leader is also a visionary:
     "Having or marked by foresight and imagination <a visionary leader> <a visionary invention>"[26]

Every leader should have a vision.

   Habakkuk 2:2–3 (NIV)—"Then the Lord replied:
   "Write down the revelation and make it plain on tablets so that a herald may run with it. For the revelation awaits an appointed time: it speaks of the end and will not prove false. Though it linger, wait for it; it will certainly come and will not delay.

II. Leader vs. manager

Definition of a manager:

   a. "A person responsible for controlling or administering all or part of a company or similar organization."[27]
   b. "A person who controls the activities, business dealings, and other aspects of the career of an entertainer, athlete, group of musicians, etc."[28]

III. The leadership call

   Self-appointed leadership: Korah (Numbers 16 and 17)

   God-appointed leadership: David (1 Samuel 16:12)

---

[24] http: //oxforddictionaries.com.
[25] http://merrium-webster.com.
[26] Ibid.
[27] www.oxforddictionaries.com.
[28] Ibid.

IV. The call of Moses, Jeremiah, and Gideon

Ephesians 4:11, 12:

"And He gave some as apostles, and some as prophets, and some as evangelists, and some as pastors, and teachers."

The call of Moses—Exodus 3:1–11

Moses' youth, his failure (Exodus 2:11–15), his stripping process

Moses' response to the call

1) The response of unworthiness (Exodus 3:11)
2) The response of fear of rejection (Exodus 3:13–16)
3) The response of unbelief (Exodus 4:1)
4) The response of a lack of eloquence (Exodus 4:10)
5) The response of inferiority (Exodus 4:13)
6) The response of unfruitfulness (Exodus 5:21–22)

The call of Jeremiah—Jeremiah 1:4–10

Jeremiah's response

1) The excuse of youth (Jeremiah 1:6)
2) The excuse of timidity and the fear of rejection (Jeremiah 1:8,9)

The call of Gideon—Judges 6:11–12

Gideon's response to the call.

1) The excuse of circumstances (Judges 6:13)
2) The excuse of no miracles (Judges 6:13)
3) The excuse of unbelief and frustration (Judges 6:13)
4) The excuse of inferiority (Judges 6:15)
5) The excuse of family background (Judges 6:15)
6) The excuse of youth (Judges 6:15)

V. Our time of testing/preparation

a) The time/patience test (waiting on God for direction and fulfillment of *His* promises)

b) The character test (temptations of all kinds)

c)   The motivation test (What motivates you to serve God? Will you continue to serve God if/when your circumstances change (i.e., family, finances, etc.), or when those who you thought would be there with you are no longer beside you?)

d)   The servant test (Are you willing to serve instead of being served?)

e)   The wilderness test (relying on God for daily manna)

f)   The frustration test (feelings of anger or dissatisfaction toward the ministry)

g)   The discouragement test (feeling as if God has forgotten)

h)   The warfare test (trials of all kinds)

i)   The self-will test (Are you doing what *you* want to do, or what God wants you to do?)

j)   The vision test (doubts concerning the ministry's vision)

k)   The usage test (feelings of inadequacy, and/or feeling as if you're not doing enough or your gifts are not be utilized in the ministry)

The preparation phase

Joshua—Was Moses's aide (Exodus 24:13)
Was one of twelve spies who saw the Promised Land (Numbers 13:30–14:9)
Was appointed by God (Numbers 27:18–23)

Joseph—Became second in command after being in prison (Genesis 39–41)

Jesus—Was led into the wilderness by the Holy Spirit (Luke 4)

Commonalities in their ministry—wilderness phase, rejection, and ministry fulfilled

VI. Warfare ministries of the leader, an ambassador of Christ

God the protector. As a covering and as a watchman, the effective Christian leader is also a refuge, a rock, a shelter, and a strong habitation.

God the defender. As a defender, the effective Christian leader is also a shield and buckler, a fortress, and a high tower.

God the deliverer. The effective Christian leader is also a deliverer, a redeemer, and an opener of blind eyes.

VII. Restoration ministries of a leader

God the counselor. The effective Christian leader is also a comforter, the leader as a long-sufferer and a listener.

God the restorer. The effective Christian leader is also a shower of mercy, a forgiver, a provider of strength, a binder of wounds, a healer of breaches, a healer of the broken-hearted.

VIII. Growth ministries of a leader

The effective Christian leader is a teacher and a guide, a representative of truth.

APPENDIX G

The Makings of an Effective Leader, Part 2

Part 2—Leadership seminar—"The Makings of an Effective Leader"

I. Definition of the term "leader"—a leader leads by guidance, by direction, or by example:

a. A person who leads or commands a group, organization, or country.[29]
b. A person followed by others.
c. "A person who leads: as a: guide, conductor b (1): a person who directs a military force or unit (2): a person who has commanding authority or influence."[30]
d. A leader is also a visionary:
"Having or marked by foresight and imagination <a visionary leader> <a visionary invention>"[31]

Every leader should have a vision:

Habakkuk 2:2–3 (NIV)—"Then the Lord replied:
Write down the revelation and make it plain on tablets so that a herald may run with it. For the revelation awaits an appointed time: it speaks of the end and will not prove false. Though it linger, wait for it; it will certainly come and will not delay."

II. Leader vs. manager

Definition of a manager:

a. "A person responsible for controlling or administering all or part of a company or similar organization."[32]
b. "A person who controls the activities, business dealings, and other aspects of the career of an entertainer, athlete, group of musicians, etc."[33]

III. The characteristics of an effective leader

a. An effective leader has the trust, respect, and buy-in of his/her people.

"Leadership is the capacity and will to rally men and women to a common purpose and the character which inspires confidence."—Bernard Montgomery, British field marshal

---

[29] http: //oxforddictionaries.com.
[30] http://merrium-webster.com.
[31] Ibid.
[32] www.oxforddictionaries.com.
[33] Ibid.

b. **An effective leader is courageous.** Joshua 1:6: "Be strong and very courageous, because you will lead these people to inherit the land I swore to their forefathers to give them."

"Courage is fear that has said its prayers."—Karl Barth, Swiss theologian

"Courage is rightly esteemed the first of human qualities … because it is the quality which guarantees all others."—Winston Churchill, British prime minister

c. **An effective leader is able to listen.** Communication is a two-way street.

"A good leader encourages followers to tell him what he needs to know, not what he wants to hear."—John Maxwell

"The ear of the leader must ring with the voices of the people."—Woodrow Wilson, American president

d. **An effective leader has a servant's heart.**

According to Rick Warren, real servants serve God with a mind-set of five attitudes[34] (taken from *The Purpose Driven Life* by Rick Warren):
1) Servants think more about others than themselves.
2) Servants think like stewards and not owners.
3) Servants think about their work, not what others are doing.
4) Servants base their identity in Christ.
5) Servants think of ministry as an opportunity, not an obligation.

e. **An effective leader is humble.**
Philippians 2:5–11 (the Kenosis doctrine)

f. **An effective leader knows how to delegate.**
Numbers 11: 4–17

g. **An effective leader has exemplary character.**
1) "Preach the Gospel, and if necessary, use words."[35] We set the example.
2) Character is more than talk. It's our walk, our actions, our daily life. We need to be men and women of our word. Leaders cannot rise above the limitations of their character. Spend time looking at the major areas of your life and see if you have cut corners, compromised, or let someone down.

---

[34] Rick Warren, *The Purpose Driven Life* (Grand Rapids: Zondervan, 2002), 265–71. Used by permission of Zondervan (www.zoncervan.com).
[35] Author unknown, but often attributed to St. Francis of Assisi.

3) "We need to be bigger on the inside."

   h. **An effective leader is open to change and growth.**

   i. **An effective leader exemplifies commitment, dedication, and responsibility (follows through when called upon, is on time for meetings, service, etc.).**

   j. **An effective leader has a teachable spirit.**

   k. **An effective leader spends time with God. (If not, you will become stale. You need fresh manna!)**

   l. **An effective leader knows when to rest.**

   m. **An effective leader knows to take time to be ministered to.**

IV. **Final Thought**—The church can only go as far as its leaders.

APPENDIX H

Exit Interview Questions

Exit Interview Questions

1. What did you like or enjoy most concerning the class?

2. What did you like or enjoy the least concerning the class?

3. In what way did the class affect you the most?

4. Was there a particular module that you liked better than the others, or found more effective than the others? If so, which one and why?

5. Was there a particular module that you liked the least, or found the least effective? If so, which one and why?

6. Will you take what you have learned and apply it to your ministry? If so, in what way?

7. Has this class strengthened your skills in interpreting scripture?

8. Do you see a difference with regard to your spiritual walk after taking this class?

9. Do you believe this class has enabled you to be a better leader? If so, in what way?

10. As a leader, would you recommend this class to other church leaders?

11. If you are currently not a leader, do you believe this class has prepared you in some way for leadership? If so, how?

12. With regard to the videos, do you see a difference in your public speaking capabilities? If so, explain.

13. Is there anything further that you believe you need to work on with regard to your public speaking capabilities?

14. Were there any challenges that tried to hinder you from taking this course? If so, what advice would you give to future students who want to take this class?

15. Is there anything that the instructor can do to help minimize these challenges? (i.e., day and/or time class is taught, etc.)

16. Are there any different teaching methods you would like to see in this class?

17. Will this class help you to reach your ministry goals? If so, in what capacity?

18. Is there anything you would like to see different concerning this class that you feel would enhance its effectiveness in the church? Or with church leaders?

19. Do you work outside the home? If so, will you be able to use what you have learned at work?

20. Do you see this class as one that can be taught and that would be beneficial if conducted at other churches?

Printed in the United States
By Bookmasters